How to Start a Telephone Answering Service

Peter Lyle DeHaan, PhD

ISBNs:

  e-book: 978-1-948082-11-2
  paperback: 978-1-948082-10-5
  hardback: 978-1-948082-20-4

Published by Rock Rooster Books

Credits:

  Copy editor/proofreader: Claudia Volkman
  Cover design: Cassia Friello
  Author photo: Jordan Leigh Photography

To all my friends in the answering service industry. I'd love to make a list, but it would be too long. Besides, I'd inevitably miss a few people, and that would be bad.

Patrons

The following companies and individuals helped cover the production costs of publishing this book. Without them, this book wouldn't be possible.

- Dan L'Heureux
- TASbiller / Randy J. Ripkey
- Amtelco
- ONE, Inc.
- CenturiSoft / John Pope
- Wayne Scaggs
- Gary A. Edwards
- Donna West / Focus Telecommunications Inc and Business Calls
- TUNe
- ASTAA and GLTSA
- Call Centre Hosting Inc.

Learn more about these supporters in the Acknowledgments section in the back of the book.

Table of Contents

Introduction

A telephone answering service (TAS) is a fast-paced, interesting business. It goes by many names: telemessaging company, teleservice call center, and telephone-answering bureau, to name a few. Regardless of what you call it, a successful, mature telephone answering service can be a rewarding and profitable business. And given recent technology advances that let users access answering service technology over the internet, entering the business is now easier and more affordable than at any time in the past several decades. The time is right; opportunity presents itself; potential beckons. Your future is here.

However, you don't want to enter the answering service industry lightly. It is a labor-intensive, technology-driven business. It also carries with it a twenty-four-hour-a-day, year-round commitment (called 24/7). But if you're ready for the challenge and have considered the cost—in terms of both time and money—to launch a successful TAS business, this book will help you start quickly and minimize costly mistakes. If you're exploring this as a potential business opportunity, the following pages will give you clarity.

Are you ready to take the first step?

Chapter One:

Let's Get Started

So you want to start an answering service. If you're reading this, you likely fall into one of four categories:

- You're an unhappy client at a telephone answering service and want to do it better.

- You're an employee at an answering service and want to go out on your own.

- You've heard that a telephone answering service is a good business to get into.

- You're exploring many business options, and an answering service is one of them.

There is much to carefully consider before launching a telephone answering service. It's a labor-intensive business that never closes. As you start your business—and until you reach breakeven, which may take a long time—you might find yourself working eighty hours a week or more, and you could even end up sleeping at work to answer those few third shift calls. This will take its toll on you—perhaps quickly; oftentimes gradually. Starting a TAS is not something for the fainthearted or those unwilling to make the necessary sacrifices and investment of time. While running an answering service, like running any business, is challenging, *starting* an answering service can be daunting.

On the other hand, owning a TAS can be a rewarding and fulfilling endeavor. First, you can experience great satisfaction by helping others, which is what you will do all day long. Second, an established TAS generates steady and predictable cash flow. Although clients come and go, most continue to use their answering service month after month, year after year. Third, a properly run and sufficiently large answering service can generate a substantial profit. Fourth, an answering service is a business you can pass on to your children or other family members.

I know you're anxious to jump into this, but it's important to cover some background first so you can see how everything fits together. To do this we must take a brief look at the history of the telephone answering service industry. Knowing the industry's past is essential to understanding its present, so let's start at the beginning.

Chapter Two:

A Brief History of the TAS
Industry

To know where you're going, you need to know where you've been. This is especially true for anyone moving into the telephone answering service industry. While this overview may be more detailed than you care to digest, it's helpful because it explains the present state of the industry and provides context for picking the right strategy to launch your answering service.

The telephone answering service industry began in the 1920s with various local entrepreneurs opening the first answering services around the United States. Although many claim to have been the first, there is no agreement on who was. We also don't know if they all learned from the first one who opened an answering service or if they each developed their innovative businesses in isolation.

Many of these early answering services focused only on doctors, others took on only commercial accounts (along with a few wealthy residential customers), and some did both. Today there are still telephone answering services that specialize in the medical field, as well as some who decline to take medical clientele, but most do both.

Because of the available tools and how the telephone system worked, each TAS client originated from the same telephone company central office, usually serving just a few exchanges (the fourth, fifth, and sixth digits of a ten-digit phone number).

Each customer had to pay the phone company to install an off-premise extension of his or her phone line at the telephone answering service. This was the least costly when the TAS was located within a contiguous block of the phone company's central office. For this reason, most answering services were located very close to the phone company.

An alternative for those not served by the same phone company central office as their answering service went by the descriptive name of "if no answer." Elegantly simple in concept, the business or doctor would give people two phone numbers. The first was the main number. Then they would say or write, "If no answer, call…" followed by the second number, which was their answering service (sometimes called an exchange). Companies would place this information on business cards and ads, in the phone book, and even on their signs.

Although needing to have and possibly call two numbers was cumbersome for customers or patients, it beat not having their call answered. This was especially true when calling a doctor in an emergency.

Some answering services would install a separate telephone in their office for each client. So if they had one hundred clients, they would have one hundred telephones in their office. This was a messy situation, resulting in a noisy environment when things got busy. As an alternative, other answering services rented cordboards from their phone company. The telephone company's own local and long-distance operators used this same equipment. Most cordboards could accommodate up to one hundred telephone lines.

Legally these were the only two options since the answering service could only use equipment provided by the phone company, which they rented by the month. This meant using a telephone (either single line or multi-line, which could accommodate up to thirty or more lines) or a cordboard or its equivalent.

This continued with little change until the late 1970s, when two things occurred. One was a court case that allowed people to buy certified telephone equipment from third-party manufacturers and connect it to their phone line. The development of the microprocessor and the first basic computers followed a few years later.

At this time telephone equipment vendors sprouted up, a few of which specialized in making equipment specifically for telephone answering services. Initially these devices were electromechanical solutions, which slowly gave way to computerized alternatives. Today all TAS systems are computer-based.

Around the same time call forwarding developed, allowing people to forward their phone calls to another number, often that of an answering service. This removed the need and expense of installing an off-premise extension. It also greatly expanded a TAS's service area to include the entire local calling area, which was far greater than just one central office. A wave of answering service consolidation followed.

Although it took several years, the internet provided the next major advance in answering service functionality and flexibility. Increasingly telephone companies digitized phone calls and sent the data over the internet or a comparable digital network. Called Voice over Internet Protocol (VoIP), it paved the way for calls to arrive over a high-speed internet connection instead of a telephone line.

A parallel development goes by many different names (and with no real agreement on the subtle differences): Software as a Service (SaaS), hosted services, cloud-based computing, and so forth. The essential element of these options is that, instead of installing a computerized TAS system in one's office (a premise-based or on-premise solution), the system's computers are located off-site in a high-tech facility maintained by the system vendor. The answering service only needs computers for its operator stations, an office network, and a reliable internet connection.

This provides three key benefits. The first is financial. Using an internet-based system negates the need to buy a complete system, instead incurring a monthly service fee. This removes the capital expense of a system purchase and replaces it with a monthly operational expense, affecting both the balance sheet and the income statement.

Second, with answering service systems growing more technologically advanced, installing equipment on-site requires a trained technical staff to maintain it. Moving to the internet removes most of the technical complexities of running an answering service, leaving only the network and desktop computers to content with.

Third, this gives answering services the flexibility to scale up quickly, move locations with ease, and allow operators to work anywhere they have a stable internet connection. There are other benefits of using a hosted answering service solution too. Today some answering services install systems on-site, and others opt for hosted solutions. Though there are valid strategic reasons for both, the trend is toward the cloud-based alternative.

In addition, the industry has been undergoing another wave of consolidation in recent years, with big services getting bigger. This means decreased competition, though it is still formidable. Despite the barriers to entry, this provides potential for answering service start-ups.

This is the current climate of the TAS industry. It's also the point where you, as a future telephone answering service owner, can enter the industry. Options and opportunities abound.

Next we'll look at various TAS business strategies and pick the ideal one for you as you start your very own answering service.

Chapter Three:

———— ⌇⌇ ————

Strategy Questions

There are two primary considerations as you consider your basic start-up strategy. The first is whether to buy a system or use a pay-as-you-go approach. We typically refer to this as the premise-based system versus hosted solution decision.

The second is whether to require your staff to work in your office or allow them to work from remote locations. We call this issue the centralized versus decentralized staffing dilemma.

Premise-Based System Versus Hosted Solution

The distinguishing characteristic between the premise-based and hosted options boils down to owning your system versus paying for access. It's a decision that involves many aspects of your business, including financial considerations and technical ramifications, along with your anticipated growth. A key issue is your own comfort level and preferred management style. Here's how it breaks down.

Premise-Based: There's something powerful in buying equipment to run your answering service and installing it in your office. It's tangible, it's present, and it's yours. It's also expensive—upwards of $50,000 to $100,000 for a good *starter* system. You buy it and that's it, aside from smaller monthly maintenance fees and occasional upgrades.

You finance the purchase, paying it back over three to five years and depreciating the purchase on your balance sheet. After paying off the loan, the former equipment payments now flow straight to your bottom line. Of course, with rapid technology advances, your system may need replacing right around the time you make your final payment. So you get a new loan, install a new system, and repeat the process.

This is what most answering services have done since the early 1980s.

Hosted: The alternative, a much more recent development, is the hosted or cloud-based solution. In this case the only hardware you'll need to buy are network equipment and computer stations for your agents. Your vendor handles the main part of the system at the datacenter, and you connect to it through the internet.

You pay a monthly fee to access and use your vendor's system, paying only for what you need, when you need it. The vendor handles all the maintenance, backups, security, and upgrades. When new features or software updates become available, you get to use them right away, usually at no additional cost.

With this approach you do not need to finance an expensive system, so there are no loans to procure or assets to depreciate. Your monthly fees show as an operational expense on your income statement, and your balance sheet remains unaffected.

Of course if your internet connection goes down, you can't access the system, but then, without the internet, you can't do too much with a premise-based system, either.

Established answering services are exploring hosted solutions as the preferred option, and some have switched over to it. For new answering services, the hosted solution is usually the best approach.

Centralized Versus Decentralized Staffing

The second consideration is deciding whether you want your entire staff working from one site or if you'll allow them to work at multiple locations, including their homes. With today's answering service technology, having staff work anywhere with an internet connection is a viable alternative. The decision to do so hinges on two things: your management style and local labor markets, with each favoring one of these two options.

Centralized Staff: The chief benefits of having your staff together at the same location include greater control and natural synergy, both of which are harder when co-workers aren't physically in the same office. The overarching factor, however, is management style. A management style that works well in a centralized environment usually falters in a multi-location arrangement—especially when employing home-based operators working in physical isolation.

Historically the technological limitations of answering service systems and telephone company offerings necessitated that staff work from a single site. Even now, with the technology barriers lifted, many answering services remain fully or mostly staffed at one location. This primarily stems from the complexities of overseeing a staff working in multiple places. Many successful one-location managers have failed when overseeing a multi-location workforce.

Decentralized Staff: The primary motivation for not having staff work from one location is usually the practical reality of finding qualified staff to answer phone calls and serve clients. Some answering services open second locations convenient to workers in a second labor market. In this case a manager or high-level supervisor oversees the staff at the second location, solving the difficulty of one person trying to manage a multi-location staff.

A common scenario occurs when a valued employee moves out of the area. To retain that employee, the answering service must allow that person to work from their new home. In this case the remote employee already has the necessary training and has proven his or her abilities, thereby earning the right to work from home.

A third scenario exists in reaching out to otherwise qualified applicants who are homebound. This may be due to physical limitations, transportation issues, emotional reasons, or other practical considerations. In any case they have limited employment options, but they often possess stellar skills and work potential. Though training such individuals presents significant challenges, once they're trained and proficient, they often stick around much longer than other employees, simply because they have fewer employment options available to them, and you have met the needs of their situation.

Still, the overriding factor is properly managing staff not working in the same location as their manager. This is a critical issue; do not dismiss it. For this one reason I would never recommend that a start-up answering service even consider the idea of remote staff—unless the manager has successfully done so in the past at another answering service.

Conclusion: I highly recommend that you launch your telephone answering service using a hosted service and keep your staff at one location. Once you have established your answering service, you can consider multiple locations, including employing a home-based staff, as well as buying your own equipment. But at the beginning it's wise to start simple with the least costly and most manageable situation. These two decisions will limit your risks in starting an answering service.

Chapter Four:

―――~~――――

Frequently Asked Questions

When you're considering whether to start a TAS, you'll have lots of questions. Here are answers to some common questions about telephone answering services. Even if the question doesn't seem applicable, the answer may contain helpful information for you.

Expected Profits

Question: Is it true that answering services generate a 30 percent annual profit?

Answer: While it is correct that some answering services generate a 30 percent annual profit or even more, they are in the minority. These typically are the larger, more established answering services that have been around for decades or at least for several years. The contributing factors to their high profit margins are their size and the owners' expertise in deftly managing the complexities of a twenty-four-hour-a-day service-based business.

Many telephone answering services, however, generate a much more modest profit for their owners. And many smaller answering services do not make much of a profit at all or even lose money, especially when they first open. These operations may not even generate enough profit to pay their owners a reasonable salary for their many hours of work, with some owners not making minimum wage or even working for free. How long can you survive without an income?

Most start-up answering services face these dismal prospects. The key to minimizing the length of time with no profits and substandard compensation is to grow quickly, provide consistent service, and build solid relationships with clientele.

Answering services can be profitable businesses, but it takes time and effort to get there.

Not an Easy Business

Question: This seems like an easy business. You just need to answer the phone and take messages. What's the big deal?

Answer: Having an inaccurate understanding of what's involved in starting and operating an answering service is the quickest path to failure. A telephone answering service is a labor-intensive, technology-laden business. And most new owners minimize these two critical realities.

When you sign up your first client, you immediately assume a 168-hour-a-week payroll. Hiring, training, and scheduling staff to fill three shifts a day, seven days a week is challenging. This means a minimum of five employees, assuming no overtime—and you never want to plan on overtime; it is bound to happen on its own unless you are extremely careful. Labor costs, left unchecked, can quickly exceed revenue—and certainly *will* exceed revenue in the early stages.

If an operator doesn't show up for their shift or calls in sick, someone must fill that shift. If the business is small, this usually falls to the owner. And every hour you spend on the phone answering clients' calls is an hour not spent on marketing and growing your business.

On the equipment side, selecting the wrong system (or the wrong features) can eat away at profits. Many start-up answering services try to get by with a cheap system, adapt non-answering service technology, or use standard telephones. These shortcuts will make it very challenging to serve your clients and will hamper growth.

If your clients have used a TAS in the past—and most have—they will come with a set of expectations you can meet only by using a system designed specifically for telephone answering services. If you fail to meet those expectations, clients will quickly leave your service for one that can provide the level of services they received in the past.

There are many areas where things can go wrong in an answering service, and a start-up is especially vulnerable to them. Staffing and technology are two key considerations.

While this book will guide you in how to minimize the risks of starting an answering service, never assume it will be easy.

Absentee Ownership

Question: Is this a good business for an absentee owner?

Answer: In the past, when answering services served their local community and had little competition, an absentee owner could get by with having a good manager to handle the day-to-day operation. If the manager stumbled or the service lagged, clients had few or even no options, so they accepted any less-than-ideal situations as unavoidable and continued to use the service.

However, with recent advances in technology, answering services are no longer local businesses serving local clients. Every telephone answering service can serve clients anywhere in the United States and even around the world. Today's market is highly competitive, and clients have hundreds of options. (If your TAS is not in the USA, refer to the final question.)

While absentee ownership could have worked in the past, today a successful answering service requires a dedicated leader in the office on a regular basis to ensure the staff is providing exceptional service, the expenses and payroll stay within budget, and the billing is proper, accurate, and collected. It's rare to find anyone without a stake in the business who will consistently handle these tasks on a long-term basis. Lacking this leadership, even a well-run TAS can crumble in a matter of weeks.

An absentee owner must have an experienced, dedicated manager in place, someone who thinks and acts like an owner. Finding and keeping such a person is difficult at best.

Free Labor

Question: I have some friends and relatives who have offered to work for free to help me get started. Doesn't this solve my labor liability?

Answer: Expecting someone to work for free—even if they offer to do so—for more than a couple of days is the quickest way to lose a friend or alienate a relative. It's also not a good business decision. If people work for free, they should receive a portion of ownership in exchange for their efforts (often called "sweat equity"). In addition there are legal considerations in such an arrangement, so proceed only after consulting an attorney who specializes in businesses.

Be sure to document any such arrangement regarding free or volunteer assistance, as misunderstandings are bound to occur. The last thing a fledging answering service needs is a lawsuit. And if you lose the lawsuit, which could happen in the absence of clearly written legal agreements, the settlement could bankrupt your business.

The best advice is to not consider free labor.

Local Competition

Question: Is it a good sign that there is no answering service in my community?

Answer: There are two answers to this question. First, there is a good reason why there is no telephone answering service in your area. Quite simply, the market may not be big enough to support it. At a minimum, your local calling area needs to be large enough to provide you with eighty to one hundred answering service accounts, and this is just to break even.

Until a few years ago this answer was the only answer. Now the situation has changed. With advances in technology, a TAS no longer serves a local market; it serves the whole country. Therefore because your market is not local, it doesn't matter where you're located—provided you can find enough qualified workers to staff your answering service. And since technology has made it possible for your staff to work remotely, you don't even need to be in a good labor market.

However, I strongly advise a start-up answering service to hire only local people who work out of one office. To do this you must locate in an area with a suitable labor pool. Also, be aware that it's easier for most salespeople to close a local sale then one in another city or state.

So the second answer is that having no local competition is still not a good sign, but it's not as detrimental as it once was.

Critical Mass

Question: How many accounts do I need to break even?

Answer: This, of course, varies with the size of your answering service accounts. Even one large account can dramatically reduce this general rule of thumb, but plan on needing eighty to one hundred accounts, each one billing one hundred to three hundred dollars a month, to reach a break-even point.

Even though one large account would change this significantly and reduce this number, it's also risky when too much of your monthly revenue comes from one source. While answering services benefit from monthly reoccurring revenue, no client will use your service forever. Every client will cancel their service at some point. This can be because their business needs change, they go out of business, someone acquires them, or they switch to another answering service that promises to offer them more than you do.

If a large client—who may comprise a significant part of your revenue—leaves, will you be able to remain viable with your remaining clients? How long will it take you to replace the lost revenue?

Reaching Breakeven

Question: How long should it take me to reach breakeven?

Answer: This depends on the effectiveness of your marketing, the tenacity of your sales, and the quality of your service. Start-up answering services *always* drastically underestimate how long it will take to reach breakeven, be able to pay owners, and eventually earn a profit. If you can't run your telephone answering service for several months (or even a year) at a loss, then you shouldn't start one.

Even if you can add one new account per business day, which is hard for most start-ups to pull off, it will take five months to reach one hundred clients, assuming no one cancels (and some will). And if by some good fortune you can sell more than one account per day, this presents a problem for operations: programing the new account, fine-tuning details, and training the staff. This all takes time.

Of course, you may not be able to add one new account per day, which will stretch out the time to reach breakeven beyond this five-month minimum.

Labor Costs

Question: How much of my expenses should go to labor?

Answer: This is an interesting question. With one hundred properly billed accounts (the target breakeven point), you can figure that approximately 60 percent of your revenue will go toward labor. As you grow beyond one hundred accounts, the percentage will decrease since you will become more efficient.

When you have less than one hundred accounts, your labor costs will not be based on call traffic (the number of calls that come in) but on the need to have one person work around the clock (168 hours a week). Even at a low wage, with minimal benefits, this results in a monthly payroll of over $7,000. In the beginning *all* your revenue will go to labor. In fact, in the beginning your labor expenses will far exceed your revenue.

Growth Rate

Question: Can I grow my answering service in a slow and controlled rate?

Answer: Not really. The day you begin answering calls for your first client, you take on a 168-hour-a-week labor liability. Conservatively speaking this requires a $7,000-a-month payroll, so you need to quickly add as many accounts as you can to cover your labor costs. Figure on needing one hundred typical-sized accounts to reach breakeven. You want to reach this number as quickly as possible.

Daytime Only Operation

Question: I don't want to offer round-the-clock service; is there a market for a daytime-only answering service?

Answer: Scaling back your hours of operation lessens your labor liability dramatically, but it also significantly reduces your prospective market. There might be only one client out of one hundred who is looking for daytime-only coverage. These accounts are hard to find. The few answering services that are only open during business hours usually do so in conjunction with another business, such as secretarial services or executive suites.

There are two strategies that some answering services use to provide twenty-four-hour coverage without staffing twenty-four-hours-a-day. The first is to revert to 100 percent automation when you receive the fewest calls, such as during third shift. With today's modern answering service systems, which include integrated voicemail software and automatic dispatching, this is a viable option—assuming your clients will accept it.

The other strategy is to outsource your slow times to another answering service. Many answering services can handle your calls for you when it's not cost-effective for you to do so yourself. It's ideal to outsource to someone who uses the same type of equipment as you do. Check with your TAS system vendor to see if they can make any recommendations about who to contact.

To outsource calls you will need to have an agreement in place that specifies when they will serve your accounts, how much they will charge, and the logistics of how to pass calls and information back and forth.

Another critical element is to have an agreement that they will not solicit or take over any of your accounts. You can't afford to have a business partner poach your hard-earned clients.

Pricing Strategy

Question: The only answering service in the area is awful. Should my business strategy be to offer better service for a lower price?

Answer: The local service may be awful because no local competition exists to keep it sharp. Once you provide competition, expect that TAS to improve its service *and* lower its rates. Conversely, the TAS may only give the perception of offering poor service. Again, once there is an alternative, that perception may change. It might be a good telephone answering service that happens to suffer from a poor reputation, primarily because there is no other local service with which to compare it.

However, the TAS industry is no longer a local business serving local customers. Whether you want to or not, your telephone answering service will compete nationally with other answering services around the country and even globally.

It's *never* a good idea to compete on price. Someone else will always offer the same service for less. The client who chooses your service based on price will leave your service just as quickly for the same reason. The best strategy is to focus on providing consistent service and great support. You can do this at either a competitive price or a premium rate. And remember, for many people, the more they pay for something, the better they believe it to be.

Used Equipment

Question: I can't spend upwards of $100,000 on a new telephone answering service system. Is used equipment an option?

Answer: Steer away from used equipment—except in two situations. The first is when the vendor provides it: reconditioned and certified, with vendor training, support, and a minimal warranty.

The other situation is if you have personal experience using and programming that exact system. But always be careful before buying used equipment. Take steps to protect yourself. Be cautious when buying used equipment from unknown individuals. A small minority are unscrupulous and will try to cheat you, provide less than what you expect, or sell you something they don't actually own. The last thing you want is for the police to shut you down and impound your equipment because the person who sold it to you delivered stolen property.

However, my recommendation is that you don't buy a TAS system, new or used. Instead use a hosted or cloud-based system, which has no up-front costs and charges a monthly fee based on usage. And at the beginning you will not use it much at all because you will have few clients.

Experience Preferred

Question: Do I need telephone answering service experience?

Answer: That's a great question. While it isn't essential to have telephone answering service experience, it sure is helpful. If you don't have it, I recommend two options: try to gain some experience yourself or hire someone who already has it (preferably make that person your first hire).

If you want to gain TAS experience yourself, the most valuable position is at the entry level: taking calls. Nothing will provide greater insight into the answering service business. If someone does hire you, don't spend time asking questions about management, marketing, and technology that no new hire would ever ask. This will tip off your boss that you aren't who you represented yourself to be. Instead just watch what happens, noting the good and the bad, the rewards and the struggles. You will learn much.

This brings up an ethical question only you can answer. If you truly tell a competitor why you are applying for a job, they won't hire you. But lying to get a job is never a good idea, either. If you mislead your competitor, they'll always remember. Even though you'll only work there for a short time, you'll compete with that company for as long as you're in business. You certainly don't need to start your new business with enemies, so proceed with care if you choose this path.

While you could apply for a management or sales position, they'll be harder to obtain because you have no TAS experience. In addition, you may need to sign a non-compete agreement, which will keep you from opening your own service or even working at another answering service.

The other option is to hire someone with answering service experience. Just make sure the individual's position with your company matches their actual experience level, not their aspirations. While an operator *could* move to a shift supervisor or trainer, making an operator the office manager or director of human resources is too big of a jump. Hire the individual for a position comparable to what they currently have. Then as they prove themselves, you can offer them opportunities to advance.

Business Experience

Questions: Do I need business experience?

Answer: Another great question! I wish I had one great answer. Instead I have two. Please consider them both.

First answer. Yes, you need business experience, the more the better. Starting and running a telephone answering service requires a wide range of skills, including leadership, management, marketing, sales, accounting, human resources, and strategic planning, as well as technical acumen and a knack for innovation. Few people who haven't run a business can claim a working knowledge in all these areas. The more experience you have, the better off you'll be.

Second answer. No, you don't need business experience to start an answering service. You are an entrepreneur, or you wouldn't be reading this book. You love to learn and will learn what you need when you need it. Yes, you'll make a few mistakes—though hopefully this book will help you avoid the key ones—but you will grow through your mistakes and become a better businessperson as a result. You will find a mentor, read business books, and take applicable classes. You will try things no one has tried before. Some of them will work, and others will fail, but most of what you attempt will bring you one step closer to the solution you seek. You have a "can do" attitude and will make your TAS a success because that's the kind of person you are. You don't need business experience; you need personal confidence.

Other Positions

Question: Aside from hiring at least five operators (to fill out a 168-hour-a-week schedule), who else do I need to hire?

Answer: At minimum a telephone answering service needs a manager, a salesperson, a bookkeeper, and a technician. Guess what? When you launch your answering service, you'll fill all these roles yourself. This means that aside from yourself and a minimum of five operators, you don't need to hire anyone else—and you wouldn't be able to anyway because you can't afford to pay their salaries. As you grow you can gradually hire for these positions. For now let's break them down by task:

Manager: Also known as the office manager or COO (chief operations officer) in larger services, the manager role oversees the day-to-day operations of the answering service. This includes hiring, firing, training, supervising, scheduling, and customer service. As you grow you can hand off these aspects of your job to other people. But it will take time to reach that point and require hundreds of accounts before the workload justifies this position and the revenue can support it. The manager role is the most critical role in running a TAS and keeping it viable as a business.

Salesperson: As the title suggests, the purpose of this role is to sell—that is, to bring new business to the answering service. This is a critical position. In the initial phase a TAS needs as many sales as quickly as possible to grow to the minimal sustainable size of one hundred accounts. After that you'll want to continue to grow, since larger operations allow for greater efficiency. You'll also need to replace lost accounts. A well-run telephone answering service should expect to lose 2 percent of its client base every month. If you lose more than 2 percent, you'll need to determine why and correct the issues.

The salesperson's goal should be to sell one new account per business day, about twenty per month. The salesperson will also need to handle marketing: placing and evaluating ads, content marketing, email marketing, and so forth. When you hire a second sales person, you'll also need a sales manager to manage both salespeople. Often the sales manager will also handle marketing, as well as do some selling.

Bookkeeper: A TAS has several accounting functions, including billing and collections, payroll, and benefits management, producing financial reports, and record keeping for tax purposes. Properly billing for services and collecting the monies owed in a timely manner is essential. Uncollected invoices can quickly devastate an answering service. Stay on top of your collections. Don't let a client string you along.

It is wise to have a CPA file your taxes, and you can outsource payroll. But you should plan to handle the rest of the accounting functions in house.

Technician: If you purchase your own equipment, you'll need a technician or a technically minded employee to maintain your system and keep it running. When your system is down, you cannot serve your clients or make money. If you follow my recommendations and use a hosted or cloud-based solution, your technical needs will drop significantly, but you will still need someone with some computer knowledge to install and maintain the operator station computers and network components.

Consistent Service

Question: You've mentioned the need to provide quality service and consistent service. What does this mean?

Answer: Every client expects you to provide quality service, and most telephone answering services make this promise. Quality is hard to measure and to prove, however. What is equally important, or even more so, is providing *consistent* service. When your service is consistent, clients know what to expect and you meet their expectations on every call. In fact it's better to provide consistently average service than inconsistently good service.

Assume that each call receives a quality score on a one-to-five scale, with five being the best. One answering service receives threes on every call. They are consistently average, without fail.

Another answering service receives varied scores, with many fives (because they strive for quality) as well as some fours, threes, twos, and even a few ones. Their average is four, so mathematically their quality is higher than the first answering service. However, clients will expect level-five quality on every call because they receive it on some calls. When they experience a level-one or level-two call, the poor quality of that call will stand out from all the others. They will remember that one poor call, not all the good and great ones. Because of these few bad calls, they will often *perceive* the quality as being lower and will be more apt to cancel their service as a result.

While I always encourage answering services to strive for quality, it's even more important to be consistent.

Having a Partner

Question: Will having a business partner increase my chances of success?

Answer: That depends on many factors, and the answer hinges on those factors. Having a partner in your TAS could be the best thing you could do to ensure success or the worst possible decision you could make, which will destroy your business. Having your spouse as your partner could magnify either outcome. To a lesser extent the same holds true for a close family member or friend.

The benefits of having a partner are many. First, you can encourage one another. If one falls, the other can pick them up. Next, you have twice the time to get things done—and you will have a lot to do, especially in the first year or so. Third, with two of you it's more realistic to work some of the operator shifts, such as evenings and weekends, when you aren't doing your other duties at the TAS. This will reduce your payroll, which will have a huge payoff. A fourth benefit is having complementary skill sets—the most ideal scenario being if one of you handles management and the other handles sales and marketing.

The risks come when partners have misaligned expectations of how much each other will work, make unequal contributions, do not define success the same way, don't match each other in their level of commitment, or have differing financial expectations or situations.

To increase the chances of success with a business partner, spend a lot of time talking these things through, planning on contingencies, determining a separation arrangement, and documenting everything. Here are the key items to consider:

Personality Assessment: Take a personality assessment, such as Myers-Briggs Type Indicator (MBTI) or StrengthsFinder, to learn each person's strengths and weaknesses (everyone has both), discover how each person deals with conflict, and get to know each other better.

Job Description: Agree to and document what each person will do (and not do).

Work Schedules: Determine how much each person will work. If one person has a nine-to-five mentality, it's best to address this in advance.

Responsibility and Authorization: Define each person's responsibilities (such as approving overtime, handling collections, dealing with complaints, filling in shifts) and authorizations (such as who can hire and fire, who talks to the media, who can spend money—how much and for what).

Ownership Percentages: Will you have equal ownership? If so, how will you resolve disagreements?

Financial Stake: Who will put up money to start the company? How much? What does each partner expect in return?

Personal Financial Situation: How long can each partner go without a paycheck? It *will* happen in the beginning. How long can each person live on savings or have someone else support them?

Sweat Equity: Will one person invest money and the other invest time, that is, their labor? How will this affect the balance in the preceding questions?

Define Success: Agree on what success looks like, both for the company and for each partner's work.

Dealing with Failure: If one partner fails at his or her work or fails to perform at all, how will you deal with this? What steps will you take to correct the problem or dissolve the partnership?

Who's the Boss? Although it's admirable to want to jointly make every decision, this isn't practical, and you'll need a means to deal with stalemates. One person needs to have the final say.

Problem Resolution: How will you deal with problems, conflicts, and differences of opinion? They will occur, so it's wise to have a plan in place beforehand.

Exit Strategy: If one person wants out or needs to leave, how will this happen without ruining the business? Usually the departing person needs to relinquish his or her ownership stake in the company, by either forfeiting it or selling it back to the company.

In situations where both partners want the other one to leave, here is an elegant solution: One partner makes an offer to buy the other out. The second partner has two options: sell his or her stake to the first partner at the offered price or buy the first partner out for that same price. There is no negotiation, which gives the first person the incentive to offer a price that is fair either way.

Multiple Partners: The preceding discussion assumes two partners, but you could bring in a third partner or even more. Each additional person amplifies all the above issues, as well as increases the potential benefits. With four people you could divide the work as outlined in the section "Other Positions," with one person each to handle management, sales and marketing, accounting, and technical support. With five partners, you could fill these four roles and have one person oversee them. Regardless of the number of partners you have, be sure to invest in ample pre-planning to increase the chances of success and minimize the odds of failure.

Documentation: Write down and mutually agree to each decision you make in your arrangement with your partners. While much of this can consist of internal documents that everyone signs, it's best to have a business attorney handle other legal aspects, such as ownership and exit strategy.

This discussion uses the term *partner* in a practical sense and doesn't imply setting up your TAS as a legal partnership. You should avoid establishing your answering service as a proprietorship or a partnership. Instead form an LLC, S-Corp, or C-Corp. Seek an attorney's advice in making this determination.

Outsource Everything

Question: Can I start a virtual answering service and outsource every aspect of it?

Answer: While this is possible, it may not be cost-effective.

The two big areas of running an answering service are operations and sales. You can outsource both.

Operations: Presently I'm not aware of any telephone answering services that market themselves as an outsourcing answering service (that is, one that does work for other answering services), but some will do this, especially for third shift. Some answering services may be open to discuss you outsourcing calls to them. The problem is margins. You'll need to charge your clients more than what your outsource answering service charges you.

While you will need to pay more for a quality outsourcer, they may be open to charge you less because they won't have any sales and marketing costs and will have minimal billing and collections work—just one bill to you.

Sales and Marketing: There are sales and marketing companies that specialize in selling answering service services to the end client. You pay them a fee, and they find you clients. They usually charge a monthly retainer and a commission for each sale. Prices vary, but don't assume this is inexpensive. You must pay for quality and speed.

Accounting and Customer Service: This leaves accounting and customer service. You can outsource these as well. But you might not be able to afford to do so.

So, yes, you can outsource everything and run a virtual answering service. The bigger question is whether you can do this and still make money. The likely answer is no.

However, strategic outsourcing or short-term outsourcing may make financial sense.

Other Countries

Question: The focus on this book seems to be answering services in the United States. What about other countries?

Answer: I address the USA for two reasons. First, most answering services in the world are arguably located in the US. And most of my experience and knowledge about the telephone answering service industry relates to the US. (Canada is very similar to the US in this regard, and European countries are comparable.) Since I don't want to write about things I don't know much about, I've chosen to focus on the US market.

If you're in a different country, I leave it up to you to apply these situations to your local circumstances and adapt them as needed to your environment. Most of the information in this book applies to any country or market. What could be different, aside from governmental issues, is the stability of internet access, the quality of the labor market (either higher or lower), the rates you can charge for your services (which affects your break-even point), and the demand for your services.

You can set up a TAS to serve your country, or you can set up an answering service in your country to serve the US market or other desirable markets. Often the reason to serve another country is tapping into a more profitable market using the cost advantages of less costly local labor. This is a viable strategy, presuming you and your staff understand the other country's culture, priorities, and practices.

Chapter Five:

———— ~~ ————

Action Plan

The first step in establishing a telephone answering service is to have an action plan. As the saying goes, failing to plan is planning to fail. Here is a basic—yet sound and reasonable—seventeen-step action plan:

1. Examine Your Motives

Make sure you want to start a telephone answering service for the right reasons and have realistic expectations. As we mentioned in the beginning of this book most people want to start a telephone answering service for one of the following reasons:

- They don't like the answering service they are using.

- They work at a TAS and think they can do it better.

- They heard an answering service is a great way to make lots of money.

The first two reasons unveil risky motives, while the third exposes a faulty expectation. If these are your reasons, be careful—very careful.

However, if you want to own a business, enjoy serving others, like to talk on the phone, and thrive in a varied and fast-paced environment, then starting a telephone answering service may be a means to tie all these things together. While doing so, you will have the *potential* to earn a good income. The chances of getting rich from owning a telephone answering service, however, are slim, but you can achieve a good living with hard work and effort.

2. Research the Industry

Knowledge is power. Therefore, the more you learn about the telephone answering service industry, the greater your chances of success. Studying this book is a key part of that process.

Other ideas include reading industry publications (see the Resources section in the back of this book), joining answering service associations, studying industry literature, and talking with answering service system vendors. The internet is also a source of information, but be careful about the advice you find there. Some sites are valuable, and some aren't. Some online information about telephone answering services is decades out of date or just plain wrong. Make sure any information you find online comes from a reputable person with current industry involvement. Most of what I've found online about starting a TAS does not meet this criteria.

Talking with owners of other telephone answering services can be most helpful. However, keep in mind that you represent a future competitor to them, so most owners will be reluctant about sharing information that could hurt their own business. If you do find an owner willing to help you, treat them with great respect and be careful not to abuse their good nature. Look for ways you can give back to them.

3. Write Your Business Plan

Having a simple yet effective mini-business plan for your telephone answering service is essential to keep you on track and focused. Unless you will borrow money or seek investors, your business plan does not need to be formal or long. If you do need a formal business plan, then read a book about doing so. There are many good resources.

In your business plan you should indicate what type of business entity you will form: sole proprietorship, partnership, LLC, S-Corp, or C-Corp. Check with both your lawyer and accountant before you make this decision, as you will need to balance their different perspectives (legal protection and tax strategy) to determine the right solution for you. There will also be licenses or permits to obtain and insurance to buy.

Your business plan must have a basic budget (sometimes called a pro forma) for the first year and rough projections for the first five. This is next to impossible since you have nothing to base it on, but do your best. Your budget should be conservative on income and generous on expenses. Also, it will take longer to reach breakeven than most entrepreneurs think.

As you complete the following steps regarding marketing, equipment, and staffing, you can continually expand and complete your answering service's business plan and budget. Remember that a business plan is not a once-and-done obligation, but a living, evolving strategy to continually move you toward success. You will want to update it often, especially during the start-up phase.

4. Determine Your Rates

The first step in determining what to charge clients is to know what your competition offers and what they charge. Sometimes this information is readily available from competitors' websites. Often it is harder to come by. If you need to dig for this information, exercise great care so you don't do anything unethical or illegal.

When it comes to determining your answering service's rates and fees, decide how you want the marketplace to perceive you as a provider: premium, high value, competitive, or low-cost solution. However, I strongly recommend against pursuing a low-cost provider strategy. If you do, know that every sale you make will hinge on price. And just as customers leave their current provider to switch to your service, they will later leave you for the same reason. Competing on price is the quickest way to lose clients and money.

Virtually all start-up answering services *dramatically underestimate* what it will cost to run their business and therefore *drastically undercharge*. This hurts both the industry and the new answering service.

When determining your rates, you will need to create a preliminary list of what services you will provide and what options you plan to offer. Knowing what services the industry offers gives you the basis for what you will need to provide to your clients. Try to match or surpass your primary competition; never offer less. Often the services offered are a function of the TAS platform they use, so this list of services will later become your shopping list when you research answering service systems.

5. Establish Your Business Entity

You had some preliminary discussions with an attorney and accountant about your business plan. You did do that, right? If you skipped that step to save money, don't persist in your frugalness. Yes, you might save a couple hundred dollars now, but that could cost you thousands of dollars later. I know; it happened to me. When setting up a business entity I followed my attorney's advice without consulting my accountant. That shortsightedness cost several thousand dollars in additional taxes the following year.

I am not a lawyer, but I do advise against setting up your business as a proprietorship or a partnership. Both options expose you and your personal assets if someone sues your answering service. Lawsuits can and do happen in this industry, and upset clients threaten to sue more often than you might think. For those reasons, my advice is to form an LLC, S-Corp, or C-Corp that will shield personal assets from business liability.

Make sure you check with *both* your attorney and your accountant. One will give you recommendations from a legal standpoint and the other from a financial perspective. Their advice may conflict, and you will need to meld their recommendations to find the ideal answer for your situation. Unless you have prior experience in setting up a business, don't use an online service to file the necessary paperwork for you. These services are mostly clerical in nature and don't provide legal or financial advice.

In addition to establishing your legal entity (with your lawyer) and setting up the basis for your accounting, payroll, and record keeping (with your accountant), these professionals can guide you in other areas as well, such as assisting you with the various licenses, permits, and paperwork you'll need to file. If you do things right from the beginning, you'll avoid unpleasant surprises later.

One thing your lawyer may not mention is "errors and omissions" (E&O) insurance. This is special liability protection insurance in addition to your normal business insurance policy. E&O insurance provides a layer of protection if someone sues you, or threatens to sue you, for a mistake you made while answering the phone, taking a message, or giving information to a caller. This also covers you for what you inadvertently fail to do, such as not reaching a client with an urgent message that results in loss of business to the client or hardship for the client's customer. A most extreme example is a patient who dies after leaving an urgent message with your answering service, but your operator doesn't contact the doctor.

While your business entity helps protect your personal assets in the event of a lawsuit, E&O insurance helps protect your business from a potentially crippling loss. If you decide to purchase E&O insurance, seek a company that has offered it to other answering services. You want an insurance company with an understanding of the unique issues faced by the answering service industry. And you need it in place before you take on your first client.

6. Launch a Killer Website

Your website is key to your success. Now is the time to plan for it and make it the best you can. Do not skimp on this step.

Your website is your online brochure, and it will be the first stop for most prospects. Think of it as your primary selling tool. If you don't wow potential clients with your website, you will lose them as prospects. You need an impressive online presence.

This doesn't mean it has to be big or fancy, but it does need to convey competence, trust, and reliability. And it can't look like an amateur created it.

Your website will require several key pages, but keep in mind, as the saying goes, "less is more." Your telephone answering service website should have:

- A compelling home page that grabs prospects' attention
- A description of the services you offer
- A commitment to quality or whatever your key distinguishing strategy is
- A "get a free quote" option
- An "About Us" feature and contact information
- A "blog" section to add content marketing pieces

Make your web content simple to understand, use eye-catching visuals, and avoid industry jargon (you probably don't know too much of that yet). Make sure it is distinctive—you don't want it to look like most of the other websites in the industry.

Invest time in studying competitor's websites. Note what you like and don't like. Look for trends to avoid and seek ways you can stand out. Use this information to plan a great website. Make sure you do this right, and don't go cheap. This means you need to hire a professional web designer. Make sure he or she understands search engine optimization (SEO)—many designers don't.

Although this is a personal preference, my advice is to ask for a site built on WordPress. Worldwide, nearly one third (32.5 percent) of websites use the WordPress platform, and the number continues to grow. Having a WordPress site gives you the most options for support (should your designer disappear or prove inadequate) and the most tools to enhance your site, which are often free or cost very little. Also, with WordPress, you can make simple changes yourself.

Once your website is ready to go live, don't delay. The longer a site has been online, the more credibility search engines give it, so get it online as soon as possible. Most people won't find it until you begin actively marketing anyway, but if they do and request a quote or more information, simply respond, "We are not currently taking on clients at this time and will contact you when we are." In doing so you can start gathering email addresses and contact information for your prelaunch marketing phase.

It's easy to procrastinate about your website, but the closer you get to your launch date, the busier you will become. So develop your website now, and make it a great one.

7. Prepare Your Marketing Materials

Sales and marketing is a critical step, and it's one where most start-up telephone answering services stumble.

A TAS is an intangible, commodity-like service that is hard to sell. Even clients who are unhappy with their present TAS are reluctant to switch because they fear the unknown and worry that the new service could be even worse. In addition, since you are just starting out and haven't yet launched, you don't even have a working operation to show them or talk about.

Once you have your website finished, add these three sales resources:

1. Business cards

2. An inexpensive, but professional-looking brochure

3. A service and price list

These three items must all match each other and align with your website. You want to portray a consistent image and a cohesive brand. You will hand these out to a few people and mail them to some others, but you will send most via email as an attachment. So make sure you have access to your brochure and price list in digital form.

8. Select Your TAS Platform

This is a critical step. Start-up systems for a telephone answering service can cost upwards of $100,000, which is why I recommend that you not buy equipment and instead use a pay-as-you-go solution (a hosted or cloud-based solution). This minimizes risk and maximizes flexibility.

The features available on the system you select will dictate the types of features you can offer your clients and what you will charge for them. The tendency is to focus on the price and features of the system, but also look at the company behind it. How long has this vendor been in business? How big is the company? How many systems have they sold? What about product support? Is there a users group?

Make sure the vendor specializes in the telephone answering service industry—otherwise what they provide will disappoint you. Don't depend on a system made for a different purpose and expect it to work for an answering service. This is seldom true and has ruined many a TAS.

When you narrow down the list of top vendors, make a point of learning more about them. You may even want to visit your top prospect. This will give you a good feel for the type of company you'll deal with. During your visit spend some time in the customer service department. These are the folks you'll work with after you select your system, so make sure you're comfortable with them. Also meet with their trainers to make sure they're knowledgeable and competent.

If there is a users group for this vendor, check it out as well. A good users group will be a lifeline to success.

Last, talk with other users of the system to see what they have to say. Their feedback will be insightful. Remember that every company has its detractors, so keep things in perspective. Your vendor should also be able to arrange for you to visit one of their customers so you can see the system in action. Take advantage of this. What you learn will be invaluable.

Once you've made your selection, ask for technical specifications needed for operator workstations, the network, and the type of internet connection required. Find out how the vendor provides training and how long the training takes. Typically a vendor will train key people and expect them (or you) to train everyone else. This all takes time.

Most TAS system vendors have an associated users group. Connect with the users group associated with your TAS system as soon as you make your vendor selection. These groups provide valuable secondary support, as well as ideas and encouragement. Some vendors control their respective user groups, while other groups function independently, but in either regard they are excellent resources. Once you join the users group, look for ways to contribute as well as receive. (Some groups also have established relationships with insurance companies that provide answering service E&O insurance.)

9. Determine Your Launch Date

The launch date for your telephone answering service is the date you plan to "go live" and begin answering calls. By then you will need your computers, network, and internet connection installed, your staff hired and trained, and most importantly a group of clients ready to use your service. We will address these in subsequent steps, but for now set a target date so that you have a goal to shoot for. Failure to set and stick with your launch date will result in costly delays and loss of respect from prospective clients who are waiting to use your service.

Have a just-in-time mentality regarding this. You want your office ready, the service available, and your staff hired and trained as close as possible to your launch date. But you don't want staff on the payroll with nothing to do, computers paid for but still in boxes, or an office rented that remains empty. Strive to coordinate all these events to converge at one point in time: your launch date.

Start by being clear about your TAS vendor's timeline, which includes service availability (usually quite soon) and training (usually a couple of weeks). For both you will need your computers and network set up. You will also need an internet connection. If you require any additional phone services, check with your phone company on installation lead times. Be aware that in too many instances an installation date does not equal a working date. That is, don't schedule a Wednesday installation if you need it working on Thursday. Assume delays.

Begin to line up clients, as well as hire and train staff. Although you should train them while they still have their current job, assume the staff you hire will need to give two weeks' notice to their current employers so they can be ready at your launch date. This means you should begin interviewing a month in advance of your launch date: one week to interview and make your selections, one week to train, and two weeks for them to give their notice.

Remember that you need to staff 168 hours a week. This will require a minimum of five employees, most of them full time. However, having full-time staff is more costly than part-time, so many answering services hire a mixture of full-time and part-time employees. While full-time employees are more reliable and long term, the payroll and benefit costs are also greater. Part-time employees offer more flexibility with lower costs, but since their job with you is often a second one, they will be less likely to stick around.

If you only hire part-time people, they will not likely be quitting another job to work for you, so allowing time for them to give their two weeks' notice becomes a nonissue. This reduces your lead time. You will also need to hire more people—perhaps eight or nine part-timers to fill the 168-hour-a-week schedule.

Keep in mind that if you hire and train staff but miss your launch date, they'll wander off to find other jobs. This is one reason it's critical to hit your target launch date.

As you do all of this, you need to be out selling and lining up clients to begin using your services when you go live. Most of those who are interested will be willing to wait a few weeks but not much more. Know that they are looking for an answering service to relieve a pain point or solve a problem, so their patience has limits. They want a solution as soon as possible, so if you start selling too long before your launch date, prospective clients will get tired of waiting and make other arrangements. Plan to allow approximately four weeks for active prelaunch sales and marketing.

Mesh the particulars of these elements together to develop a timeline and project your launch date. Keep in mind that you can only do so much, so don't over commit yourself.

10. Begin Your Prelaunch Marketing

When your launch date is a month away, it's time to begin prelaunch marketing. The goal is to have clients lined up to begin service on your launch date, the more the better. If you have followed this timeline, you already have basic marketing resources: business cards, a brochure, and a price list. Your effective, compelling website is up and running.

If you skipped these steps or put them off, you aren't ready to market your TAS, and so you aren't a month away from launching. Put your schedule on hold. Go back and do your marketing prep, and then set a new launch date. Your prelaunch marketing should include the following checklist:

Set up a LinkedIn page: Of all the social media platforms, LinkedIn is easily the best for connecting with other business owners (potential clients). The page should be complete, highlighting you and your career. List your current employment as president or owner of your answering service. Then connect with everyone you know, especially business owners and managers. You want to begin establishing yourself as the go-to person for all things answering service-related.

Your goal on LinkedIn is to make connections and interact with people. It is *not* to sell. It is for building relationships and contributing to the online community you are establishing. The closest you should come to selling on LinkedIn might be asking your network, "Do you know of anyone who needs a telephone answering service?" This is a much softer approach then saying, "Do you need a telephone answering service?"

Once you've mastered the basics of LinkedIn, dig deeper. There are plenty of books and online classes about successfully using on LinkedIn.

I don't see the other social media platforms offering much benefit to growing your answering service. Though you should set up a Facebook page to give information about your answering service, don't expect too much from it. Only a very small percent of the people who like your Facebook page will see what you post—unless you pay a fee to boost viewership.

However, if you feel you've mastered a social media

platform and can reach and engage an audience, then pursue it.

Make a list: Start with business people you know who need (or use) an answering service. Add to it any interested leads your website has generated. As you talk to people about your answering service, some of them will want to learn more. Make a list of all these people, along with their contact information. You will use this list for follow-up work and email marketing.

Do some email marketing: Consider starting a newsletter to email potential clients. Take advantage of the many books or classes that specialize in email marketing and e-newsletters. This is a low-cost marketing solution. The one key thing to keep in mind is to never add someone to your email-marketing list who hasn't given you permission to do so. This is not only a bad business practice, it's also illegal.

Begin content marketing: Basic content marketing consists of blogging with the primary goal of providing useful information to your target audience. The indirect goal is pointing them to your business or establishing yourself as a TAS expert.

Post these content marketing pieces on your website and promote them on LinkedIn, your Facebook business page, and any other social media platforms you may have. Some people like to post their content marketing pieces directly on social media sites, but I recommend that you merely reference them on social media and direct traffic to your website.

Read up on content marketing if you aren't familiar with it. Also, if writing isn't your thing or you lack the time to do it, consider outsourcing this.

Follow up with prospects: Begin contacting your prospects. Your goal is for them to start service with you on your launch date. Selling will be even more challenging at this point because you don't have a working office or any clients who can vouch for you. Be patient and diligent. Don't let discouragement overtake you or start selling with a tone of desperation. Some of your prospects may be ready to commit in time for your launch date, but most will take longer, sometimes much longer.

Ask every prospect if you can add them to your email list. This way you can keep in touch with them when you send each newsletter.

Conduct Online Marketing: Use online marketing to drive people to your website, with the goal that they will request more information. Remember, I said your website needed "a compelling home page that grabs prospects' attention." This is the reason. Your ads should point people to your home page or a specific landing page.

An ad is effective if people click on it and go to your site. Your site is effective if they request more information or a quote. And you are effective if you close the sale. When you analyze the effectiveness of your online marketing efforts, know the purpose of each element so you can determine what's working and what's not.

Online marketing can be a quick way to spend a lot of money and end up with nothing to show for it. So start small, test carefully, and limit your daily expenditures. If you aren't familiar with online marketing and don't want to waste money as you learn through trial and error, do your homework, and read up on it first.

Optional Marketing Strategy: The various aspects of these steps can be daunting. As an alternative you can outsource much of the sales and marketing tasks by hiring an answering service sales and marketing firm.

This is a great solution for building your client base quickly—usually much quicker than you could do on your own. These firms typically charge a monthly retainer, and then you pay a commission on each sale. Keep in mind that good firms with the ability to produce great results will charge fees that match their expertise.

11. Find a Location

You likely have a location for your telephone answering service in mind. This is a step many people do too early. However, if you don't yet have a location, now is the time to find one, negotiate the terms (rent, sublease, or buy), and sign the paperwork. If possible, delay the actual start date (that is, the time when you must begin making payments) until the week your equipment arrives, you've scheduled your internet installation, and you plan to begin interviewing operators.

Unless it is integral to your business plan, you don't need a visible or prestigious location. Clients typically won't visit your office, although some local ones might want to check things out beforehand.

There is, however, one primary location consideration, and it's critical. Your office must be accessible to your target labor market. This includes being near mass transit systems and main thoroughfares. Convenient parking for your staff is a nice bonus. Of paramount importance is choosing a safe location in a secure area. If employees are afraid of the neighborhood or fear for their safety, it will be difficult to hire and retain good staff. Remember that, as a twenty-four-hour-a-day business, you will have staff coming and going at all hours. They need to be safe.

12. Order Your Internet Service and Computer Hardware

Your vendor can recommend the type of internet connection you need to have as well as the specs for the operator station computers and network you'll need to purchase. Order these according to your launch timeline. You will need your office space lined up prior to this. And you must do these steps before training your operators, so plan accordingly.

You'll need at least three computers: a primary operator computer, a backup computer, and a computer for all management functions. As the name implies, the backup computer is in case something happens to your primary operator computer. Expect that you will periodically need to use your backup, even if only for a short time. You can also use the backup computer to add new clients and make changes to accounts. The backup computer also could serve as the management computer for sales, marketing, billing, and accounting functions, but I recommend having a separate one exclusively for management use.

First install your operator station computers and network. The amount of time needed for this will depend on the configuration of your office and any requirements dictated by your landlord. You should have these up and running prior to the installation of your internet connection so you can test the internet using your computers and network.

Assume that your internet access may not actually work on the day you order it. It may take an extra couple of days before it is ready to use.

If you need any phone lines installed, now is the time to order them.

13. Connect to Your Vendor's System

Once you have your operator stations, network, and internet access, you'll be able to connect to your vendor's system. They'll instruct you how to do that. They may provide training online, or they may send a trainer to you.

If the vendor sends a trainer, block out your entire schedule to focus on training. You'll need unrestricted time with no distractions to maximize the learning experience. They may train you and then expect you to train everyone else. Or they may train you and a few key people, assuming you have hired anyone at this point and they're available for training when the trainer is there.

Whatever you do, don't skip the training yourself; don't have someone else receive the key training in your place. If that person leaves or does a poor job at training others, you'll be left without a backup plan. You must know how to operate all aspects of the system. Your business is at stake, so master your system.

Learn all you can while the trainer is there. Not only do you need training on how to take calls, but also on how to program the system and set up accounts. Be sure to take notes—do not rely on your memory. There is a great deal to learn in a short time.

Your vendor may provide manuals or give you access to them online. However, despite most vendors' best efforts, their manuals and documentation are seldom up-to-date. Assume this is the case with your vendor, so take good notes.

14. Hire and Train Your Staff

Once you have an office—and concurrent to ordering and installing your system—you can begin interviewing and hiring your operators. Remember that to staff around the clock (twenty-four-hours a day, 168 hours a week), you will need five people—and up to eight if you hire part-time staff.

While you can take a regular shift yourself to save money, this will also lessen the amount of time you can spend on sales and marketing. Though you can handle many marketing activities between phone calls—since you won't be receiving many calls in the beginning— the one thing you don't want to do is follow up with prospects when you are also working as an operator. It is unprofessional to be talking with a prospect and then put them on hold to answer another client's line. They'll wonder what kind of operation you're running. Segregate operator work from making sales calls. Do these two tasks at separate times.

Before you can train your operators, make sure your computers, network, and internet access are working, and you have mastered the training yourself. Plan on a minimum of one week to train your staff. You can do this one-on-one or in groups, providing you have one agent station for each person at the training session. Since most people learn by doing, each person will need to be at an operator station computer during training.

Set up test accounts to use for training. It's even better if you have lined up clients to start service on your launch date—you can use their accounts for training. In this way you can learn how to operate the system and become familiar with your new clients at the same time. However, if you use real accounts for training, be sure to delete all messages and clear out their statistics before you begin taking real calls.

15. Setup Your Accounts

As you sign up new clients, enter their information into the system. You'll want to set some programing parameters to govern basic functions for the account. Most of these will be standard for all accounts, so make a list for handy reference. Part of the account setup establishes what your operators see when they answer the line and take messages. It is key to follow a consistent format, so all accounts look the same. This will help your operators be more efficient and reduce errors.

Your vendor can offer suggestions as to what this format could look like. But it's unlikely you'll find the ideal layout from the start, so expect to fine-tune this over time. Just remember to keep all the accounts looking the same.

16. Begin Serving Your Clients

Now everything is in place, you have clients lined up, and your launch date has arrived. At last you can begin answering and processing calls for your first clients. Congratulations! You have successfully launched your telephone answering service.

17. Optimize Your Operation

The next goal is to grow your telephone answering service as quickly as possible to reach the break-even point. Your ongoing objective is to continually fine-tune, improve, expand, and grow your new TAS business. This will continue for as long as you are in business.

Optional Approaches

There are two alternatives to starting a telephone answering service from scratch. The first is buying an established answering service and the second is outsourcing the phone-answering portion to someone else. As small businesses go, running a TAS is both labor-intensive and capital-intensive. Therefore anything you can do to reduce either concern will minimize the risk of starting an answering service.

Buying an existing telephone answering service provides you with an existing, viable client base to begin generating revenue immediately. Sometimes the purchase will entail only the clients, whereas other times you can buy the entire system and assume the existing staff.

Alternately you can outsource the call-answering portion to another TAS that specializes in this service. You will still do all the sales and marketing, customer service, and billing, but the other company will answer all the calls, deal with labor issues, and maintain the equipment. Outsourcing can be a short-term solution until you reach a critical mass of clients, or you might choose to adopt it as your long-term strategy.

Of course you can do both: buy the client base from one answering service and then outsource the labor to another. If you pursue either or both scenarios, you will be able to skip some of the preceding steps, at least for now.

Glossary

You may wonder why this book has a printed glossary when this information is available online. There are three reasons.

One, these definitions focus specifically on telephone answering services, whereas online information is general and might be confusing. Next, some information online is out-of-date or wrong. Third, the internet provides a lot of information to wade through, which can waste a lot of time.

This resource will get you what you need fast and from one place. Start here and then go online if you want to dig deeper.

You'll encounter these words in the TAS industry. Some of them are becoming obsolete, but they're included so that when someone uses them, you'll have a basic understanding and context. It also includes some relevant telecommunications and computer terms.

The key words you should know are italicized. Focus on them and save the rest for later.

24/7: notation to indicate continuous operations, twenty-four hours a day, seven days a week, said as "twenty-four-seven." Most telephone answering services (and outsource call centers) operate 24/7. Other notations include 24/7/52 (for fifty-two weeks a year), 24/7/365 (for 365 days a year).

66 Block: passive device that provides a connection point for telephone lines and trunks. Often split in the middle (a "split block"), the two sides connect using bridge clips. The bridge clips serve as the point of demarcation ("demark") between the telephone company and the customer's equipment.

ACD (**Automatic Call Distributor**): device that routes and delivers incoming calls in call centers to agents. Compare to switch and PBX.

Agent: generic name for call center employees, encompassing both CSRs (Customer Service Representative for inbound calls) and TSRs (Telephone Sales Representative for outbound work). The common label used in the answering service industry is *operator*.

Analog: signal (or voltage) that can vary continuously between two limits. Contrast to digital, which possesses only two states or conditions. Speech is analog, though modern communication systems convert it into a digital signal for transmission, switching, and storage.

ANI (**Automatic Number Identification**): telephone company service that provides the telephone number of the calling party (and sometimes the caller's name) electronically to an answering service (or call center). It's a more sophisticated version of caller ID.

Answering Service: see Telephone Answering Service (TAS).

Area Code Overlay: assigning one area code to supplement another. An area code overlay occurs when assigning a new area code to the same geographic region as the existing area code(s), which is running out of numbers (number depletion). With an overlay, no one needs to change area codes. However, if not already implemented, ten-digit dialing becomes required for all calls, even local numbers. All new number assignments are in the new area code. As such, ordering a second line could result in a number with a different area code. Overlays are not popular with most consumers, as they don't want to dial ten digits on every call, nor remember different area codes for friends and neighbors. Overlays *are* popular with most businesses since it doesn't require them to update their literature, advertisements, and website with their new area code. Contrast to an area code split.

Area Code Split: dividing an area code in parts, usually two. An area code split occurs by dividing the geographic region of the area code in two. One part will keep the same area code, while the other section must switch to a new one but retains the existing seven-digit number. There is a transition period for this, called permissive dialing, in which users can dial either the old or the new area code. At a certain point, mandatory dialing goes into effect, and any call to the new region using the old area code won't work. These numbers eventually become available for reuse. Area code splits aren't popular with most businesses because it requires printing new stationary and other changes, as well as reprogramming phone systems. To avoid repeating this process in a few years, sometimes a three-way split occurs. Contrast to an area code overlay.

ASP: acronym for Application Service Provider; refers to a company that makes software available via the internet. The ASP handles maintenance, upgrades, and backups. End users pay a fee to use the software. Newer terms for this concept are SaaS, hosted solutions, and cloud-based solutions.

Asterisk: open source telephony software that emulates the functions of a private branch exchange (PBX) and uses Voice over Internet Protocol (VoIP) services, including SIP. Some TAS (and call center) industry solutions are Asterisk-based.

B Channel: part of ISDN service, the B channel, also called the bearer channel, carries voice transmission. In BRI-ISDN, there are two B channels, whereas in PRI-ISDN, there are twenty-three B channels; all B channels use 64 kbps of bandwidth.

BA: see Business Associate.

Bridge Clip: small conductive metal device used to electrically connect a phone line from one point to another. The bridge clip is used on a split block and is the demark point. Removing the bridge clip disconnects the telephone company and customer equipment from each other, isolating them for troubleshooting.

BRI-ISDN (Basic Rate Interface ISDN): simple version of ISDN that provides two main channels for voice, fax, or data and one data channel (primarily for control purposes). See ISDN; compare to PRI-ISDN.

Bureau: older, less common name for a telephone answering service.

Business Associate **(BA)**: part of HIPAA, a person or organization that performs a function or activity on behalf of a covered entity (CE). Medical telephone answering services are BAs, and their clients are CEs. Also see PHI.

Callback: call center service where people waiting on hold (in queue) can request that the call center call them back when it is their turn. Alternately a callback is a website feature that allows a user to submit a request for an operator to call them. Compare to the "talk-to-me" feature, which uses VoIP to establish a phone connection over the internet.

Call Center: a centralized location that receives, answers, and processes calls. In common usage it also covers *decentralized* operations. Although call centers were around prior to the 1980s, the industry commonly uses that timeframe as the start of the call center industry. Although answering services preceded the call center industry by several decades, an answering service fits within the definition of a call center. *Contact center* is a broader term, often substituted for call center.

Caller ID: service that provides the telephone number of the calling party to the called party. See ANI.

Call Forward-Busy Line: variation of call forwarding where a call forwards only when the line is busy. This is a great way to get overflow calls to an answering service. Businesses often use it in conjunction with call forward-don't answer.

Call Forward-Don't Answer: variation of call forwarding where a call forwards only when the line remains unanswered for a certain time, with six seconds equaling one ring. Therefore if you order three rings, it will forward after 18 seconds, regardless of where it is in the ring cycle. There are two limitations with call forward-don't answer. First, in most cases, you can't change the "ring count" quickly, as it often requires placing an order with the phone company. Second, once a call forwards (that is, the ring count has been reached), the client can no longer answer it in their office. It's often used with call forward-busy line or as a backup to regular call forwarding in case the client forgets to activate it. You can override call forward-don't answer with regular call forwarding.

Call Forwarding: telephone company service that allows calls to one number to automatically redirect to another number. You can forward calls to either a local or long-distance number. In either case the line with the call forwarding incurs the cost (if any) of routing the calls to the other number. When a phone is call forwarded, it usually rings at the main location to indicate that call forwarding as occurred. Users can't answer as it forwards but can still make a call from a phone with call forwarding activated. Most answering service clients use call forwarding to redirect calls to their answering service.

Call Recording: see voice logging.

Card: portion of computer equipment containing circuits and components, which users can easily remove and replace; also called a circuit card or printed circuit card.

CE: see Covered Entity.

Central Office (CO): telephone company facility that connects customers' lines to switching equipment so they can call other numbers, both local and long distance.

Chat: internet-based service that allows two or more users to type messages to each other. Chat is a real-time communication; compare to email, which is not real-time communication. Sometimes called text chat.

Client: customer of a telephone answering service (or an outsource call center).

Cloud: system for interconnecting computers and computer systems around the world to share and send information. At its most basic, the cloud is synonymous with the internet.

Cloud Computing: internet-based computing service that provides shared resources to users over the internet. Increasingly answering services (and call centers) use cloud-based systems. Sometimes called on-demand computing; see hosted solutions.

CO: see central office.

Commercial TAS: telephone answering services that handle only commercial clients and don't take on any medical clients. Though some answering services do only one or the other, most do both.

Conference: procedure to connect three or more people together on a telephone call, allowing them to talk simultaneously with each other. Compare to patching.

Contact Center: newer name for a call center, reflecting that other forms of contact (email, fax, text chat, internet callback) are handled in addition to phone calls.

Covered Entity (**CE**): in simplistic terms, an entity that transmits protected health information (PHI) under HIPAA regulations. Contrast to a Business Associate (BA), who performs such a function on behalf of a CE.

CRM: customer relationship management, which seeks to properly oversee and direct a company's interaction with its customers. CRM can refer to the concept or the tools to implement it. See customer experience.

CSR (Customer Service Representative): employee of a call center tasked with providing phone support to customers who call for assistance. See operator and agent; contrast to TSR.

CSU/DSU (Channel Services Unit/Digital Services Unit): device that interfaces equipment to a digital circuit, typically T-1 or ISDN. It offers protection and serves as the demark and diagnostic point.

CTI (Computer-Telephony Integration): computer system integrated with a telephone switch to present relevant computer database information about the caller or client to the CSR simultaneously with the call. The telephone answering service industry enjoyed basic CTI functions with its first computerized systems in the mid-1980s, years before the general business market had the technology. Now, more sophisticated CTI platforms are common, representing the leading edge of technology.

Customer Experience: overall results of an encounter that a consumer has with a vendor over a particular transaction or over the customer's entire lifecycle. See CRM and customer satisfaction.

Customer Satisfaction: assessment or a measurement of how pleased customers are with the service they receive. This can occur through surveys or informally through self-reporting.

D Channel: D channel in ISDN service, also called the delta channel, handles control and signaling functions. In BRI-ISDN, the D-channel is 16 kHz of bandwidth; in PRI-ISDN, the D-channel is 64 KHz.

Decision Tree Software: computer software program that presents a series of predetermined questions, each based on the answer of the previous question, allowing agents and operators to reach a correct decision even though they may not personally have the expertise required to make such a determination. Properly configured decision tree software enforces consistency and reduces errors.

Dedicated 800 Service: the opposite of switched 800 service, which permanently connects toll free numbers (800, 888, 877, 866, 855, 844, and 833 prefixes) to the customer's switch, usually via T-1.

Demark Point: point delineating the answering service's (or call center's) responsibility from the phone company's. For basic telephone services a split block provides a connection point for telephony lines, with the two sides connected via bridge clips. The bridge clips serve as the point of demarcation ("demark") between the telephone company and the user's equipment. Removing the bridge clip disconnects the telephone company's lines and the user's equipment from each other to allow for troubleshooting and testing. More sophisticated telephone service, such as ISDN, DSL, and T-1, also have a demark point, such as a CSU/DSU or modem.

DID (Direct-Inward-Dial): telephone service, pronounced "D-I-D," in which there is no direct relationship between a line and a specific telephone number, but where many numbers route to one trunk or a group of trunks to increase efficiency. The phone company identifies the called number by repeating the last few digits of the number prior to sending the call. DID service only receives calls. However, some phone companies have enhanced DID service allowing users to make calls on DID trunks as well. This allows for greater efficiency (serving two purposes) and a higher quality patch (since the phone company's central office handles the connection). Called two-way DID, this isn't available from all phone companies.

DID Numbers: group of usually consecutive numbers, often in multiples of twenty or one hundred, used for DID service. The numbers have no unique physical line, and calls cannot be placed on a DID number.

DID Trunks: physical lines that DID calls use. Many DID numbers can be handled on a few DID trunks. Although phone companies and telephony engineers often recommend ratios as low as one trunk for each six numbers, the common reality for the answering service industry is a much higher ratio of 1:25.

Digital: representing information in a two-state format, either "on" or "off," 1 or 0. Computer programs, information, and instructions all exist in digital form. Speech, although an analog waveform, is converted into a digital format for transmission or storage (such as in a voicemail system). The transmission and switching of speech in digital form provides greater overall quality than analog. Most modern telephone switches are digital switches and represent improved quality over older analog switches.

Digital Switch: device that directs or routes calls; it processes all phone calls digitally. A digital switch is more advanced and produces higher quality connections that are less prone to noise. Virtually all switches on the market today are digital switches.

DIP (Dual-in-line-package) Switch: series of miniature switches, all housed in the same unit, used in computer and telephony systems to set options. Compare to jumper.

Distributed Call Center: By definition a call center is centralized, so to distribute its functionality across multiple locations seems like an oxymoron, but today's technology allows that to happen, with call center agents able to work from any location that has internet access.

DNC: acronym for do not call; not to be confused with the Democratic National Committee. See do not call.

Do Not Call: legislation dictating who telemarketers can call and when, often shortened to DNC. The federal government passed DNC legislation in 2003, and some states have passed more restrictive laws. The DNC legislation was in response to the abuse and overuse of some call centers that aggressively called and even harassed consumers.

The national DNC legislation also established a DNC registry, where consumers can opt out of receiving telemarketing calls. (Businesses cannot opt out.) Offenders can receive severe penalties and fines, with repeated infractions amounting to millions of dollars. Interestingly, one of the exceptions carved out in the law allows for political calling.

The DNC laws almost wiped out the outbound telemarketing industry, and those call centers that remain must go to great lengths to conform to and obey these laws. Often they rely on third party providers who specialize in following DNC regulations to ensure their clients' compliance.

DS-1: see T-1.

DS-3: see T-3.

DSL (Digital Subscriber Line): transmission protocol that sends high-speed data over standard copper wires. There are several different types of DSL service, such as ADSL and VDSL, each providing different transmission speeds. People sometimes use DSL for internet access.

DTMF (Dual-Tone, Multi-Frequency): method of placing a call using a unique pair of tones to represent each digit of the phone number. Also known by the AT&T registered trademark of touch-tone.

E-1: European counterpart to T-1, E-1 is a designation for a high-speed, four-wire data circuit that can accommodate up to thirty-two separate audio channels.

Employee Satisfaction: assessment or measurement of how pleased employees—specifically TAS operators—are with the work they do, their work environment, and the rewards they receive, both tangible and intangible.

Flat Rate Service: phone company designation to indicate an unlimited number of local and/or long-distance calls included in the monthly service fee. Compare to measured rate service.

Firmware: software contained on a computer chip, such as a PROM or EPROM.

Gamification: applying the elements of a game to employees (such as operators) as they work or to customers as they interact with a company. For both groups gamification can increase engagement, improve satisfaction, and lengthen tenure.

Gateway: passage between two computers, programs, or systems that allow them to directly share information. Gateways facilitate computer communication.

Generator: device that produces electricity to run equipment in the event commercial power is lost. Powered by gasoline, propane, or natural gas, generators produce AC power to run electrical equipment. Generators provide power long-term, while UPS (Uninterruptible Power Supplies) systems provide immediate, short-term power. Most answering services (and call centers) use both a UPS and generator to provide uninterrupted, long-term power.

Gigabyte: measurement of computer memory capacity, a gigabyte is one billion bytes of data or 1,000 megabytes. Sometimes incorrectly shortened to "gig" or "gigs."

Gigahertz: measurement of transmission frequency, either over the airwaves or through a fiber optic or network cable. One gigahertz is one billion times a second, or 1,000 megahertz.

Headset: hands-free device allowing operators to talk on the phone and keep both hands available for typing. Headsets are essential for TAS operators (and call center agents).

Headset Box: network interface device into which operators plug their headset. A headset box connects to the phone system (PBX, ACD, or switch). Some equipment allows for a direct headset connection, usually a computer, without needing a headset box. Today many operator headsets directly plug into their station computers.

Help Desk: segment of the call center industry where agents answer questions and provide basic customer support functions for technical applications.

HIPAA: acronym for the Health Insurance Portability and Accountability Act of 1996, which among other things addresses the privacy of health information and has wide-ranging ramifications to the medical community in general and medical answering services (and healthcare call centers) specifically. See CE (covered entity, BA (business associate), and PHI (protected health information).

Hosted Solutions: system housed in another location and shared with other users who access their partitioned portion of the system through the internet. Other common names include SaaS (software as a service) or cloud services. Though some argue for subtle differences between each of these terms, most people use them interchangeably. Increasingly TAS (and call center) applications are hosted services. Compare to premise-based systems.

Inbound Telemarketing: one of two forms of business telephone contact, where customers or prospects call a company for assistance at their convenience as opposed to outbound telemarketing, where the company calls customers or prospects.

InterLATA: between LATAs (local access and transport areas). InterLATA call traffic consists of calls going from one LATA to another. See LATA and contrast to IntraLATA.

Internet: complex international network of networks used to send email and information from one computer to another. Several different services are available on the internet, including email, accessing websites, and voice communication.

Internet Telephony: see VoIP (voice over internet protocol).

IntraLATA: calls that stay within the same LATA (local access and transport area). See LATA and contrast to InterLATA.

IP Telephony (Internet Protocol Telephony): see VoIP (voice over internet protocol).

ISDN (Integrated Services Digital Network): international standard for an all-digital telephony communication service. There are two types: BRI-ISDN and PRI-ISDN.

IVR **(Interactive Voice Response)**: computerized system that allows callers to interact with and receive information from a database using touch-tone signals. Text-to-speech conversion provides information to callers. Some IVR systems also recognize basic speech instead of requiring callers to press keys on their telephone.

Jumper: mechanism used on printed circuit cards to provide basic operating settings. Generally this consists of a small metal connector, covered with plastic and designed to slide over two pins on the printed circuit card. DIP switches accomplish the same purpose.

LAN: acronym for local area network, such as one in an office or home; often simply called network. Modern TAS (and call center) equipment usually connects to a LAN.

Landline: dedicated telephone line at a business or residence. The opposite is mobile (cell phone). Though landline was the only option for telephone service for a long time, mobile is taking over for the residential and consumer markets.

Last Mile: referring to the final leg in connecting a home or business to the public switched telephone network (PSTN). Traditionally handled via a pair of copper wires, it can also be via coaxial cable, fiber optics, or even wireless transmission. Although newer technologies exist in central offices and in distribution networks, the last mile is often the final element to receive an upgrade. See local loop.

LATA (Local Access and Transport Area): historically the geographic area in which the local phone companies could handle calls without assistance from long distance companies. In many cases the LATA was the area code. However, with area code splits and overlays, this oversimplification has lost its accuracy. A LATA serves as a legal limitation as opposed to a technical constraint.

Live: an inane term to indicate calls processed by a real person as opposed to automation from an IVR platform, voicemail system, or answering machine. Although call automation is preferred in some circumstances, most consumers prefer to interact with a person trained and empowered to assist them.

Local Loop: connection between the local phone company and a business or residence. This is comparable to but more encompassing than the last mile.

Measured Rate Service: phone company services that counts (measures) and bills each local call to the calling party. Businesses in many areas are on a measured rate, though some enjoy a flat rate service that allows unlimited local calling without incurring an additional charge.

Medical TAS: Telephone answering services that handle only medical and healthcare related clients and do not handle any commercial clients. Though some answering services do only one or the other, most take both medical and commercial.

Megabyte: measurement of computer memory capacity; one million bytes of data. Often incorrectly shortened to "meg" or "megs."

Megahertz (MHz): measurement of transmission frequency, either over the airwaves or through a conduit such as a wire or fiber optic cable. Also a measurement of clock speed on a computer. One megahertz is one million times a second.

Modem: device that sends digital information in analog form over regular (analog) phone lines. Technically, a modem is an electronic device that MOdulates data into an analog signal and DEModulates it back to digital.

Multichannel: term, often used interchangeably with omni-channel (though experts like to argue about their meanings), that encompasses multiple communication options (channels) between a company and its prospects. A holistic call center (contact center) must address all these channels, not just telephone calls.

Network: interconnection of computers that allows for information access and sharing. See LAN (local area network) and internet (worldwide network of networks).

ODBC: acronym for open database connectivity and a database standard. Any database that is ODBC-compliant can connect to any other database that is ODBC-compliant.

Omni-channel: see multichannel.

Operator: common term for someone at a telephone answering service who answers calls, takes messages, and distributes those messages. Other labels are customer service representative (CSR), telephone secretary, tele-receptionist, and agent.

OPX (Off-Premise Extension): service that presents an extension of a phone line at a different location. Once this was the only method of connecting clients' phone lines to their answering services; now call forwarding is the connection method of choice.

Outbound Telemarketing: one of two forms of business telephone contact, where the company calls customers or prospects (often when it's inconvenient) as opposed to inbound telemarketing, where customers or prospects call a company for assistance when necessary. In outbound telemarketing, a company (or the call center it hires) calls consumers or businesses to make sales, set appointments, provide information, and conduct surveys. Due to abuse and overuse, laws (primarily DNC) now greatly limit who telemarketers can call and when. Contrast to inbound telemarketing, which faces far fewer restrictions.

Offshore: moving service provision to another country. For the TAS (and call center) industry, this involves relocating a US-based operation to another country, often to save money or tap into a desirable labor market. In the past many companies moved operations (mostly call centers) offshore too quickly or without proper oversight. The customer backlash was severe, and many companies have since brought the work back to the United States. Many people mistakenly think offshoring and outsourcing are synonymous; they aren't. See outsourcing.

Outsource Call Center: call center that provides various call answering and call processing services to third parties for a fee. Sometimes called a teleservice company or a service bureau, this concept applies to telephone answering services, but few people use the phrase in this context. See outsourcer.

Outsourcer: call center that processes calls for other companies.

Outsourcing: taking internal company functions and paying an outside firm to handle them. Outsourcing can save money, improve quality, or free up company resources for other activities. Outsourcing first occurred in the data-processing industry and has since spread to other areas, including call centers. Outsourcing is a growing trend. Contrast to offshoring.

Patch Panel: interface allowing for the easy connection of telephone lines or computer network wires using short cables. A patch panel saves time and money when installing or reconfiguring telephones or networks.

Patching: connecting two callers together. Compare to conference.

PBX: phone system with many of the same capabilities as a phone company's central office; sometimes called a switch. Older, larger businesses may have a PBX. Contrast to ACD, found in many call centers.

PCI DSS: acronym for Payment Card Industry Data Security Standards, a required data security compliance program. PCI DSS applies to any entity that processes, stores, or transmits credit, debit, or other payment cards, regardless of the number of transactions. This is a critical issue for any answering service (or call center) that handles credit card information for its clients or its clients' callers.

PHI: protected health information; any information relating to a person's health status, healthcare, or payment for healthcare. See HIPAA, CE, and BA.

Port: generic name for the portion of a card or system that connects with a line, trunk, network, or computer peripheral.

POTS (Plain Old Telephone Service): traditional phone service found in some homes and businesses, now often called a landline. POTS contrasts with services such as ISDN, T-1, DSL, and VoIP, which are digital, provide greater bandwidth, and offer more features.

Power Down: to turn off the power. Users power down a system to replace a card or component or troubleshoot issues. Turning the power on, or powering up, will cause the system to restart or reboot.

Power Supply: component in computers and switches that converts 120 Volts AC (alternating current) to the DC (direct current) voltages required by the unit to operate. Some computers or switches connect directly to DC power, requiring an external DC power source.

Premise-Based Systems: system installed on-site, compared to a hosted system, which is located off-site. Historically answering services used premise-based technology, though the trend is moving toward hosted solutions.

PRI-ISDN (Primary-Rate Interface ISDN): high-capacity version of ISDN that allows for twenty-three main channels (for voice, fax, or data) and one data channel (primarily for control purposes).

Printed Circuit Card or Board: card containing electronic circuits and components to perform specific functions. Printed circuit cards and boards are common in computers and switches.

PROM (Programmable Read Only Memory): see firmware.

PSTN (Public Switched Telephone Network): traditional international telephone system in which phone calls are switched or routed from origin to destination.

Queue: number of calls on hold or ringing as callers wait for the next available operator (or agent). Most telephone answering services (and call centers) use a queue; it allows for increased operator efficiency and greater productivity.

Remote Operators (**Remote Agents**): TAS (and call center) staff that does not work at the main office but at a remote location, such as a satellite office or from home. Easily accomplished with hosted services and cloud-based solutions.

Rep (Representative): alternative name for agent or operator; see CSR and TSR.

Restart: force a component to re-initialize itself by reloading software, clearing memory, or some similar function; effectively the same as boot, reboot, or reset.

Ribbon Cables: flat, ribbon-like cables used to connect different components or boards in a system.

RJ-11 (Registered Jack 11): standard modular jack used to connect a single phone line. In alternate variations, it can also handle two or three lines.

RJ-45 (Registered Jack 45): standard modular jack used for computer network connections. It accommodates eight wires.

SaaS: acronym for software as a service; sometimes called software on demand. The concept is licensing software on a subscription basis. Vendors centrally host the software in their datacenter. Increasingly TAS (and call center) applications follow the SaaS model. See hosted solutions.

Screen Pop: causing a computer to display information about the call at the same time the agent or operator answers it; a feature of CTI (computer telephony integration).

Secure Messaging: protects sensitive information, such as financial data or health records, from interception or unauthorized access, as opposed to insecure information transmitted through the internet or over the airways and available to anyone with the technology to access it. Secure messaging is especially important for medical answering services (and healthcare call centers) to be HIPAA compliant.

SIP: session initiation protocol, a communications protocol for internet telephony, both voice and data, using internet protocol (IP). Increasingly telephone answering services (and call centers) use SIP instead of older telephony technology such as DID and ISDN.

SMS: acronym for short message service, such as text messaging on a smartphone, Web, or mobile device. See chat.

Social Media: internet-based platforms for sharing information and connecting with others on an egalitarian, peer-to-peer basis. The amount of information shared and warranting a response on business social media pages provides service opportunities for telephone answering services (and call centers).

Softswitch: using software to switch phone calls, as opposed to older electromechanical analog and digital switches that accomplished this using a combination of software and hardware.

Speech Analytics: software that automatically analyzes recorded calls to mine call information. When this happens in real-time, supervisor intervention can intervene on calls that aren't proceeding well.

Speech Recognition: software that recognizes spoken words and can provide user verification and speech-to-text applications. IVR systems sometimes use speech recognition to allow callers to say their response as an alternative to entering it via a keypad. For example, "For customer service, press or say one."

Split Block: see 66 Block.

SS7 (Signaling System 7): sophisticated telecommunications protocol that provides out-of-band signaling and data interface between phone company switches to reduce congestion in the PSTN (public switched telephone network). For example, without SS7 a long-distance call routes through the network to the called party to make their phone ring or return a busy signal, thereby tying up circuits along the entire path. With SS7 the data interface sends a message to the end switch to ring the phone or check if the called party is busy before routing the call. If someone answers, the call immediately routes through the network, thereby not using the circuits while the phone is ringing or in busy and no-answer situations.

Surge Suppressor: electronic device that limits the damaging effect of power surges on electronic equipment from commercial power plants, generators, and electrical storms. All critical equipment should plug into a surge suppressor.

Switch: generic name referring to any device that can connect and route calls, either analog or digital. Digital switches are more advanced. They produce higher quality connections and are less prone to noise. Analog switches are older technology and not used much today. See ACD and PBX.

Switched 800 Service: long distance phone company service that routes toll-free calls (800, 888, 877, 866, 855, 844, and 833 prefixes) to existing local telephone lines; efficient and cost-effective for low volume applications. Since toll free numbers do not typically have call-forwarding features, forwarding switched toll-free calls occurs by forwarding the local lines they ring in on. Contrast to dedicated 800 service.

T-1: in common usage a designation for a high-speed, four-wire data circuit that can accommodate up to twenty-four separate communication channels. Technically T-1 is the medium and DS-1 (not to be confused with DSL) is the format, though many use the terms interchangeably. A T-1 circuit is also a high-speed internet connection.

T-3: in common usage a designation for a very high-speed, four-wire data circuit that can accommodate up to twenty-eight T-1 circuits (672 separate communication channels). Technically T-3 is the medium and DS-3 is the format, though many use the terms interchangeably. A T-3 circuit is also a common connection to the internet backbone.

TAS: acronym for telephone answering service and usually pronounced "tas," though some people do speak each letter. See telephone answering service.

Telco: short for telephone company.

Telecommunications: communications via telephones.

Telecommuting: allowing employees to work from home occasionally, on a regular basis, or full time. Telecommuting saves time and expense for the employee. In many cases it increases productivity, since workplace distractions don't exist at home, though other distractions may. Many employees desire telecommuting, whereas employers are more cautious.

Telemarketing: sales and service conducted using the telephone, divided into inbound telemarketing and outbound telemarketing.

Telemessaging: term some answering services use to describe what they do; the act of answering a call, taking a message, processing that information, and relaying it to the client.

Telephone Answering Service: business that handles calls for clients from a central location. They answer calls, take messages, or provide information, and then document and relay the results to the client. Many telephone answering services also offer voicemail service as well as more specialized call center services.

Telephone Triage: service provided by some healthcare call centers whereby licensed nurses talk with callers who have health concerns. Telephone triage is both a service to patients and a cost-saving tool for healthcare providers, who can direct people to the most cost-effective healthcare solution for their situation. Telephone triage call centers sometimes work with telephone answering services that screen calls or take preliminary information for the triage nurses.

Telephony: term referring to telephone lines, trunks, circuits, related equipment, and the information (voice, fax, and data) transmitted over them; of or relating to the telephone.

Telephony Switch: see switch.

Teleservice Company: see outsource call center.

Test Set: device to access and test telephone lines. Also called a butt-set.

Text Chat: see chat.

Text-to-Voice (Text-to-Speech) Software: software that converts written words into spoken words, such as reading a computer file to a user. In the call center text-to-voice software accesses information from a database and speaks it to the caller, such as "Your current balance is…" Contrast to voice-to-text.

Touch Tone: dialing method that uses tones as opposed to dial pulses, from a rotary dial phone. Touch tone is a trademark of AT&T; the generic name is DTMF (dual-tone, multifrequency).

Troubleshooting: methodical process of identifying and correcting problems with computers, telephone systems, and related equipment. Vendors of TAS (and call center) equipment provide customer support staff to help customers troubleshoot technical issues.

TSR (Telephone Sales Representative): term used in the telemarketing and call center industries for employees who proactively place calls to customers or prospects to obtain data, share information, or sell products and services. Some define TSR as telephone *service* representative, though CSR is a more universally accepted term for that context. See operator; contrast to CSR.

Unified Communication: system that allows for the reception, storage, and retrieval of voicemail, email, and faxes from a common system using various interfaces, including a phone, fax machine, or computer.

UPS **(Uninterruptible Power Supply)**: device that supplies continuous power to computers and switches by converting energy stored in batteries to 120 Volts AC. Commercial utility power charges the batteries. In the event you lose utility power, a UPS provides power until the batteries run down, commercial power returns, or a generator starts up. In many installations, a UPS provides short-term coverage and gives time for the generator to start and stabilize, powering equipment during prolonged power outages. Most answering services (and call centers) use both a UPS and a generator to provide uninterrupted, long-term power.

Vendor: In the telephone answering service industry, a company that provides the system or platform (equipment and software) to run an answering service. In the call center industry, a vendor can also refer to an outsourcing call center.

Voice Logging (**Voice Recording**): recording phone calls in a TAS (or call center). Voice logging is useful for call verification, training, and customer service resolution. In the event of a lawsuit the recordings can serve as evidence, usually vindicating the answering service but not always. Most systems record only operator phone calls, whereas others record all audio continuously. Some systems link recordings to call data and even screen displays to provide a complete picture of the phone call. Laws regarding the legality of voice logging vary from state to state and country to country, as well as industry to industry.

Voicemail: device that plays announcements to callers, records messages, and allows for message retrieval. There are many different voicemail systems, each with slightly different features and user interfaces. Many newer voicemail systems provide aspects of unified messaging, which handle voicemail, email, and faxes on one platform. Initially voicemail systems were separate pieces of equipment that interfaced to answering service equipment. Today voicemail is often integrated into TAS (and call center) systems.

Voice-to-Text (Speech-to-Text) Software: software that converts the spoken word to text. Although not 100 percent accurate, a high degree of accuracy occurs in advanced systems, provided users have clear diction. Contrast to text-to-voice.

VoIP (**Voice over IP or Voice over Internet Protocol**): sending voice or phone calls over the internet. Also referred to as Internet Telephony or IP Telephony.

Work-at-Home: conducting work from one's home instead of commuting to an office; sometimes called telecommuting. Modern TAS (and call center) systems make it technologically easy for operators (and agents) to work from home.

Workforce Management (WFM): directing the activities of employees, such as operators (and agents). At a basic level this involves properly scheduling shifts according to projected needs.

Workforce Management Systems: technology to assist or automate scheduling operators and directing related activities.

Resources

Here are some helpful publications to consider:

- TAStrader.com focuses on the needs of the telephone answering service industry.

- ConnectionsMagazine.com is the premier call center magazine.

- AnswerStat.com is the information hub for healthcare contact center news and resources.

- MedicalCallCenterNews.com covers medical call centers, including medical answering services.

See more industry resources in the Acknowledgments section.

Acknowledgments

I sincerely thank the following people and companies that have helped cover the production costs of this book. Without them, this book wouldn't be possible.

Dan L'Heureux: "The TAS industry has provided a lot of jobs and revenue for those who take the risk of entrepreneurship. There is a right way and less than optimal way of doing most everything. Hopefully you will apply this book's ideas and be successful. I wish you the best in business."

TASbiller / Randy J. Ripkey: TASbiller is a popular billing program used by telephone answering services since 2000. It is recognized for its ease of use and for its profitability analysis tool. Randy Ripkey, the creator of TASbiller, is now developing an even more powerful cloud-based product for the industry. Learn more at www.tasbiller.com.

Amtelco: Amtelco's mission is working together to provide the very best communication product solutions, backed by the best support. Listening closely to the needs of customers inspires Amtelco's innovative solutions. For more than forty years, Amtelco has developed reliable new systems and applications, backed by the company's dedication to customer support.

ONE, Inc.: ONE (formally Call Center Sales Pro), founded by industry veteran Janet Livingston in 2014, is a premier business solutions provider specializing in providing human and technology-based solutions to optimize business systems and processes on a global scale. See how they can help you become a leader in your space: https://ONEmvt.com.

CenturiSoft / John Pope: Answering services provide personal service from real people, but automation plays a key support role, including voicemail, notification, escalation, and voice-delivery services. CenturiSoft (www.centurisoft.com) provides this automation for clients. This frees up operator (live) resources, allowing them to concentrate on answering calls for clients and to focus on caller needs.

Wayne Scaggs: Wayne Scaggs bought Tascom in 1994 and re-engineered its legacy system to better serve answering services. Among many innovations, he later introduced Alston Tascom's hosted system, which revolutionized access to answering service technology and solutions. On behalf of all Alston Tascom customers, Wayne welcomes this book's entrepreneurs into the industry.

Gary A. Edwards: Edwards Answering Service Enterprises has been in business since 1954. "The most important piece of advice I can give a new answering service owner is to make connections with other answering service owners. Yes, technically we are competitors, but the knowledge most of us are willing to share is invaluable."

Donna West / Focus Telecommunications Inc and Business Calls: Donna West is a tireless industry advocate, teaching answering service supervisors how to do their job with excellence. In 1987 she founded Focus Telecommunications Inc (www.focustele.com), serving as president. She also writes newsletters for answering services to send to clients (www.businesscalls.biz). In 2018 she received the ATSI Lifetime Achievement Award.

TUNe: Telecommunications Users Network, TUNe, is an association of Telescan equipment users. Members get the best return on investment from their business through networking and the opportunity to communicate with other people who understand the industry. The knowledge and years of experience among its members is immeasurable. Visit them at www.tunegroup.org

ASTAA and GLTSA: Atlantic States Telephone Answering Association, ASTAA (www.astaa.org), is an association dedicated to the education and promotion of industry best practices. Great Lakes TeleServices Association, GLTSA (www.gltsa.org), strives to provide quality education materials and networking opportunities to its members. Though initially regional groups, both now welcome members throughout the United States.

Robert Ernst / Call Centre Hosting Inc.: Call Centre Hosting provides integrated solutions and support to small and medium-sized answering services: A hosted answering service that only requires an internet connection for use, it's ideal for start-ups.

About Peter Lyle DeHaan

Peter Lyle DeHaan knows what he's talking about, having owned and managed answering services, bought and merged them, and moved and optimized them. He has managed the customer service department of an answering service vendor, coded software, and provided technical writing.

Over the years Peter has offered his expertise to the industry as a consultant to help answering services grow and optimize their operations. He has also served on the boards of industry associations.

With a PhD in business administration, Peter researched the industry for his PhD dissertation, as well as for his Master's thesis. Currently he is the publisher and editor-in-chief of the leading industry publications, *TAS Trader* and *Connections Magazine*.

Peter Lyle DeHaan knows the TAS industry and now freely shares his knowledge and years of experience with you in *How to Start an Answering Service*.

Learn more at PeterLyleDeHaan.com and PeterDeHaanPublishing.com.

Made in the USA
Las Vegas, NV
19 July 2024

92624970R00069